Patrice,

Knowing you ~~ ~~ has been like a dream, a dream I never want to awaken from. May our roads travel together, becoming one road. A road of happiness, a road of hopes; a road of love, I feel deep down my wishes came true. Thank you for coming into my life.

Richard "Evo" Love

The Evolution of One

by

Richard Brintel Lowe

Bloomington, IN   Milton Keynes, UK

authorHOUSE®

AuthorHouse™
1663 Liberty Drive, Suite 200
Bloomington, IN 47403
www.authorhouse.com
Phone: 1-800-839-8640

AuthorHouse™ UK Ltd.
500 Avebury Boulevard
Central Milton Keynes, MK9 2BE
www.authorhouse.co.uk
Phone: 08001974150

First published by AuthorHouse 4/25/2007

ISBN: 978-1-4343-0256-4 (sc)

Printed in the United States of America
Bloomington, Indiana

This book is printed on acid-free paper.

This book is dedicated to:

My beautiful little girl Brintelzya Lowe and the person who holds the key to my heart LaShunda Thomas

Contents

Acknowledgments

To God for blessing me with the gifts I have. For allowing me to over come all the challenges that were put before me.

My mother Murlin Irons. Thanks for raising me the way you did. I learned a lot from you. Your wisdom I know at times I don't care to hear it, but you have always been right. Love you.

My sister Shacara Adams. I love you girl. Thanks for hearing me out too many times to say. You have been the perfect sister for me.

LaShunda Thomas. Girl I don't know how my life would be, if I had never met you. Every time I am around you my soul is at peace and nothing, but smiles covers my face. You are beautiful and I hope you stay in my life forever. I love you so much.

Tim and Keyon Martin. You two are more than just my friends. You guys are my brothers. Thanks for being there for me, for all these years.

Monique Jackson. Girl you got mad skills with a pen, thanks for all the input and advice.

Marisa Scott. I thank you so much for the cover design. You are so bless with your skills.

All brothers and sisters: Tiffany, Sidney, and Alisa.

My Dad Roland Lowe.

My Family and friends. The men and women of the US Armed Forces.

Marisa McFarlane. For all the help you have gave to the homeless, you have touch so many lives girl. I love you for that, keep your heart where it is.

LOVE

A Girl Like You

A girl like you, is what I dream of
A girl like you, is like an angel from above
If I can soar the skies
It will be you on my mind,
Dreaming of the moments, to stare into you eyes
You're like the angel, that meets you at heavens gate
I can tell by your smile that love lies in your wake
I can tell from the things you like, that we can relate
Like the smell of roses, you bring a smile to my face
You're the real reason why beauty is what it is today
A girl like you, with such a beautiful soul
From the moment you spoke, my heart was sold
And the feeling I get from knowing you, will never get old
Like the soothing sound of waves at the beach
When ever I'm around you, my mind is at peace
I can see why woman envy your style
By trying to mimic, your beyond perfect smile
There is one thing that even a blind man can see
What your name means to me
You're like the drug that gets me high
You're like the light in my sunshine
You're like the joy in my excitement
Like the president, I will be your personal agent
When I say you're beautiful, that's more than a statement
In today's world that is what we called a fact
I just want you to know I will always have your back
So I will end this here by being very true
I am more than happy, that I met a girl like you.

All I Want Is You

All I want is you
I life long dream that came true
A girl whom I can say I love you to
A woman that knows how I feel
A woman that knows love is real
A woman that knows my deepest desires
A woman whom my heart truly admires
A woman that keeps a smile on my face
A woman I can call everyday
Before I met you I had given up on life
But you showed me the way, by being my guiding light
The more I look into your beautiful eyes
I see more and more you are meant to be by my side
So become my Nubian Queen
And love me as you King
I promise all doors can be open with true love
By being there every time push comes to shove
So now you know you are all my wishes come true
Just say yes, that you want it to be me and you.

Can I

Can I be your dreams come true
When you wake up can I be the man by your side
When you're cold can I be the one that keeps you warm
When you're sad, I promise to put a smile back on your face
Unlike most people I see your beautiful mind
I see your spirited heart
And your oh so playful ways
Your charm alone has made me fall hard for you
Someone told me the ground doesn't move
But you seem to sweep me off my feet every time I lay my eyes upon you
You have a all the elements that makes up the perfect woman
Even if I dreamed, I couldn't dream a better woman than you
So as I sit waiting to see the sparkle in your eyes
To see your smile one more time
To just hold your hand
And tell you how much you mean to me
To tell you something I should have told you long before
I love you
I love you for the woman you are
Love you for the way you make me feel
I have loved you since you help free me, from my pains
I will love you for your soul
Because, your soul is like my........ Universe.

Can I Be The One

Can I
Can I be the one
The only one in your life
The man by your side
The one your heart loves
Because I want to love you back
And so much more
I want to know all your dreams
So I can start making them come true
I want to know your desires
So I can learn to please your soul
So can I
I mean, can I really
Be your man
Because I have passion that burns for you
A passion I can no longer control
Because I want to hold you
And kiss you all over
And pleasure you with my exotic thoughts
My thought that I know will cripple you with ecstasy
I wait with this passion
That I know can complete us both
So can I
Can I...be your man.

Can You

Can you do for me, the way I do for you
If you won a getaway, would you think of me too
Can you also, be the person of my dreams
If someone says soul mate, do you think of me
Can you always keep a smile on my face
When you hear my name, does your heart starts to race
Can you be the cloud that showers love on my soul
Will your love for me ever get old
Can you be the reason, I live to see each day
When I need you the most, will you come my way
Can you show me, what true love is supposed to be
Can you promise, nothing will come between you and me.

Crazy In love

I know you think I'm crazy and I think you crazy too
You think you love me and I think I love you
I'm here to love you girl
Now that you are a part of my world
My friends call me Evo, but you can me Rich
I plan on being the man, that your heart forever cherish
The first time we met I was hooked
On how beautiful of your eyes and smile looked
Since then our love has blossomed, like flowers in the spring
And since I have earn your love, I feel I can do anything
There is not a moment that goes by when you are not on my mind
Because, I'm your Tarzan coming to save you from a vine
My love for you is flowing like a raging river
And call me your mailman of love, because I will always deliver
Call me the eraser, because I will erase all negative doubts from your head
And take all those doubts you have and make them into trust instead
I love you so much, that I can taste it
My love is so original, that my name is written on caves in hieroglyphics
Saying how we feel is always allowed
Because, that is the only way we can ever work things out
My dreams are no longer dreams, but my reality
Because I have you, a girl with my same mentality
We are together and I think it's more than a coincidence
Because the love we share is pure essence
So yeah I'm crazy, crazy about you
So just admit yourself, that you are crazy for me too.

Day Dreams

What are dreams, are they what they seem
Now imagine me
You and I on the beach
Kissing each other with a pure passion
That is forever lasting
That is blasting
An emotional climax
Between me and you
As our hearts flow through and through
With all the romantic things we do
I sense you desires in your eyes
As I kiss you on your sexy thighs
Leaving your mind feeling exotic and memorized
So as you beg me for more
And tell me how it's my licking style you adore
As your blood pressure soars
As you feel the ways of my gifted tongue
And your g spot is getting this crazed sensation
You now grab for my pants, telling me you want some
You are now throbbing wet with ecstasy
Waiting so patiently
Now begging me
For me to stick it in
So that your true pleasures may began
You feel as good as you taste
And I will be your king ready to obey
Any and everything thing you say
As I feel your warm walls around me, as I go deep in you
I know realize a feeling like this was truly meant for us too
That way you got me shaking, is to good to be true
As you pull me tight and moan my name

Screaming you love this and do I feel the same
I notice your eyes was rolled to the back of your head
I wanted to go slow , but you yelled faster instead
And you began saying, just how much you love me
And you yell out...baby I'm coming
So at that moment I was definitely at my best
And getting a nice firm grip on your breast
Saying I won't stop until you have climax
You close your eyes as you let out a loud moan
But when you open them you realize I was gone
And you were not on a beach, but in your bed alone
Day dreaming about what a man like me can do
If a modern day Romeo like me got his hands on you.

Dream Come True

I never had a dream come true
Until the day I lay my eyes upon you
You are of a perfect beauty
The complete model of what a woman should be
Like my sun shining high in my sky
You turn my darkness into light
And I pray you can be the woman by my side
Like a dream come true
I can't seem to keep my mind off of you
Thinking of how I can keep that smile on your face
So that I can have a reason to speak to you everyday
You have the perfect combination of mind, body, and soul
You're the real reason why romantic stories are told
You have more than a sexy body; you have a beauty mind
And I want you to be the woman I wine and dine
Like a single rose growing in a field
Your charm sticks out because you know how I feel
At this point I will do anything you ask
Because for you, I will always be at my best
The love I will give to you, will not be a loan
And as long as you keep me in your heart you will never be alone
So click your heels three times and you will see
That I can also be the person…. of your dreams.

Eyes

Hey pretty lady I have been admiring your smile, eyes, and style. As sit there being shy, wishing I was another guy, to come sit by your side. Your pretty eyes got me so memorize and I say to myself why, why the girl with the pretty eyes and smile, that got me going so wild. Like a cool breeze you got me in chills, wondering if you notice me. I never give myself the benefit of the doubt, I just seem to just X myself out right away, whenever I see a girl with a pretty face. Your face is uncanny, a true eye candy, but I know your are more then looks, you're the type that stay in the books. A college girl earning a degree...man please I know you are every man's dream. All I can do is just keep being me and try to speak, to you, the girl with the pretty eyes, the one I wish was mines...but for now I will let time, do it's thing and one day I will learn your name, but for now I will call you Sky, because like the stars...your eyes shine.

From The Moment We Met

Before we met, I thought life had it out for me

My invisible enemy I can feel, but not see

I felt my life was finally at its end

Than I met you a new life for me began

My cloudy days seems to have blown away

I now live to see your smile everyday

I'm now glad I have you in my life

It is you, my heart thinks of day and night

Now that I have met you, I have learned to smile

And I now know, you are what I've been searching for a while

Your eyes and smile is so beautiful to me

The image of what an angel is suppose to be

I will never hurt you and that I swear

I will continue to prove to you how much I care

I was reborn the second your lips touch mines

I pray our feelings turn to love and out last the hands of time

So thank you for being the woman you are

Because, I have found a place for you in my heart

I will always be there and never leave from your side

Because, I feel we were meant to be, I can see it in your eyes.

Hear Me

Hear me
If I call will you answer
Does it really matter I'm a libra, instead of a gemini, leo, or cancer
If someone speak of my name
Will you smile, as if I was associated with money and fame
Can you be the woman I charm
Can you be the one that melts in my arms
If I always greeted you with a kiss
Will you tell me everyday, I'm the one you were meant to be with
Hear me
As I call out to the woman of my dreams
The one who will love me for me
My angel I know you are out there
I'm waiting to spoil you and that I swear
That missing key in my life where are you
My heart is waiting to be unlocked, so that it can be just us two
When that day comes when I can stare into your eyes
I will show you what true love is morning, noon, and night.

How Can I

How can you love someone, but that don't know it
How can you have something so close, but, can not have it
How can I began to tell her how I feel, she mean the world to me
How can I get her to notice me, beyond what we are now, just friends
How can the girl of me dreams, not be in my arms
How come the woman I dreams of, don't know the feelings my heart bare
How can I be the man that keeps the sparkle in her eye, like that of a sunshine
How can I be the man she grows to love, like the way I love her
You are the one I have grown to idol
The one that sticks out, above all
The one whom manage to keep a smile on my face
The one that listen when I had tears in my eyes
The one that always stuck by my side
The one whom I know will do anything for me
Just listen to my heart beat
For it beats your name scores of times a day
Now I sit her with my feelings in disguised
Because I'm am to afraid to approach you to say what's on my mind
Just keep being the woman that you are.
And just maybe one day, you will give me that call,
To let me know that you love me from the bottom of your heart.

I Will

For you I will
For thy heart I will fulfill
For thy love
I will be the one you hug
For thy smile
I will do all I can to make your dreams worthwhile
For thy heart
I will charm it like thy melody tunes from Mozart
For thy love
I will treat you like a true angel from above
For thy kiss
I will honor you like a Nubian princess
For thy happiness
I will do things for you that are priceless
For thy to be in my life
I will make you the addiction that gets me high
Like a kite flying high in the sky
I will began and end each day with you on my mind
Like that of a sunset and a sunrise
I live to see the beauty in your eyes
I want to be the one you embrace
When it comes to you, there are a thousand words I can say
I just want you to be the one I love, honor, and obey.

Just One More Moment

I just want one more moment...one second
To hold you in my arms
To smell the beauty of your essence
To stare into those angelic eyes
To cherish your blushing smile
To feel the warmth of you kiss
To hear you say, you love me
Because one more moment with you
Would be like and eternity of happiness
A feeling that I can't put into words
But only express, with the love I have for you in my soul
My love, you are my angel
My sun that brightens my days
The stars, that sparkles in my skies
You are my universe...
And everything around me, reminds me of you
I just want one more moment with you
Times seems to pause when I have you in my arms
It may seem like a second to you
But it's a life time for me
Just the memories alone that I have for you
Would be enough to permanently put a smile on my face
I love you my angel
Until I see you again, our special moments
Will play over and over in my heart.

Like I Can

You don't know any man
Who can love you for who you are
Who can kiss you in ways you have never been kissed
Who respects your mind, body, and soul
And man who dreams to make love to you
On the beach at night
Or by stream in a valley
You don't know one man
That can touch you in ways you dream to be touched
Who listens to the words you speak
The way I can make you my angel
The way I can make you feel
I can show you love in so many ways
I can find unique ways to put a smile on your face
I can be your dream come true
I can be the lips that touches yours
I can be the eyes that call you beautiful everyday
When it comes to you my love...my angel
You will never meet a man, that will truly love you like I can.

Like You

Like beauty, you are what I see
Flawless...
An untouched beauty
But your beauty is beyond visual
It's inter…
Your mind is like that of an angel
Sense I have known you; you have charmed my ways
With just one smile, I felled for you
Your presents in my life, is like the motor that powers me
Your inter beauty is so uplifting to me
Like that, of the wings of a bird
Carrying my heart to a newer and higher limit
Feelings a sense of rejoice
I now thirst for your passion
To truly experience the love, from a woman like you
So, now as your love touch and fill my life
I thank God for blessing me with a woman like you.

My Love, My Lady

As I walk thy fields looking for thy lady
To hold in thy arms
I search for you my lady
I pray for you my lady
For it is your heart that I wish to charm
My lady whom left thy feeling so sad and sorrow
Each day for me ends wishing I can see you tomorrow
Back in my life
For thy can stare upon thy lovely eyes
My heart cries for you
Beating hastily to lay thy hand upon your face
For it is you my lady
For it is you my love I wish to embrace
I beg with tears in my eyes for you my love
My other half to return to me
How much longer must I wait
Must I plead
To have thy angel back cuddling with me in thy fields
To hear thy angel signing again in thy hills
It is your angelic voice that thy miss the most my love
And it is you that will always be my angel from above
So thy sit here with nothing but faith
To have you my love, return to me one day.

My Thoughts of You

My thoughts of you are…
Like that of a mystical sunrise
I dream to see it, like I dream to stare you into your eyes
You have this aurora about you that attracts me
Like the nectar of flowers that attracts bees
How can a woman like you, flawless as I can see
Fill my heart with hope, when I felt it was empty
I can feel your motivation and kindness flowing through me like the wind
You looked past my outer appearance and saw a real man
A man with a heart always ready to lend the first hand
So with these gifts that no one truly sees
I will write about how a girl like you saw the real me
Right now it seems we are hundreds of miles apart
But, I will reserve a spot for you in my heart
Until that day come again that I can look you in the face
You will be the only woman, I think of everyday.

Real Love

Real love
An endless surge of emotions
That flows through the veins
That can be feel with a pulsating pulse
A feeling of ecstasy
Knowing you have it
It being real love
The love that soul mates share
Love that is infinite
Like a two halves to a circle
They complete each other
True love is having that trust
That bond
The respect
The feeling of true love
Is like power
The energy that powers your heart and feelings
True love
Having the perfect romantic partner
A person that always have that perfect touch
Because real love is exactly what it is
Real, pure, and unconditional
When you are loved your soul is at peace
And you always have the smile
Because you know you belong to someone
Someone who truly loves you for who you are
A person that loves you for you soul
Because when your soul is loved
It can only be real love.

Remember

Angels come, angels go, you are who I'm still thinking of. Your angelic eyes, your wonderful mind, you are the one I want to have by my side. Your special ways, I remember those days, when we use to sit, laugh, and play. You are the key to all my dreams, caring, compassionate, and loving, is what your name means. I remember the times you told me you cared or the times I needed you the most and you were there. Do you remember those nights when we went to the movies, when I would cleverly try to pull you towards me or all those times we talked on the phone, saying how much it sucks to be alone. I remember those times staring into your eyes, saying to myself how much I wish you were my sunshine. You always knew how to use the right words, like a bolt of electricity giving me the right surge, just remember how we bring a sparkle to each others eyes and remember this always. I will not rest, until your mines.

Second Chance

For you I feel
I feel a sensation flowing through me
As my heart beat
Hoping to find your rhythm
As I lay here on this pillow
With nothing but mental
Thoughts flowing through my head
As I toss and turn on this bed
With all this misery
That is killing me
Because I have came to realize
Without you by my side
I'm just a man
That is a begging for another chance
To have you back in my arms
To feel the goodness of your charm
To feel the wetness of your kiss
Because with all of this
I just beg for your forgiveness
To love you once again
Because I love you more then I did back then
I wish you could understand
That I need to be freed from this hell
And impel
The pains inside of my heart
And promise to do my part
To keep a smile on your face
Because on this day
I will express how I feel
Because what I feel, is real
And you deserves to be truly love

And hug under the stars above
With a man that is truly meant for you
So what can I do
To find that chemistry we once shared
And escape from these times of despair
And get back to the way it use to be
When I was the man that made your life lovely
Because I feel I want to be loved again
So will you give my heart a second chance.

Secret Admire

I have a secret for you, if you don't mind
On how I won't rest until you're mines
I see you but do you seem me
I'm hooked by your shear beauty
Your eyes sparkle like the stars
You smile is perfect by far
I wish to kiss you softly upon your neck
I wish to feel the soft firmness of your breast
I wish to feel wetness from your lips
I wish to taste the cherry between your hips
I want to be the source of all your desires
I want to be the passion that your heart admires
I want you to experience the affection from my romantic mind
It will feel like love, ecstasy, and climax combined
I want to whisper love poems in your ear
Making your mind believe I was Romeo, from a play by Shakespeare
I want to please you until your eyes roll and your toes curl
And lay under the stars until our love unfurl
I know this is something your soul desires
But I will remain a secret, sign your secret admire.

Shatter Dreams....

Your heart live in either your dreams
Or this sad place called reality
I have never truly met my soul mate
A woman I feel can take my breath away
But it all change one day when I was doing what I did best
Writing of course on how I feel life is a test
This girl was not like any girl I have run across before
She was like an Angel that you will meet at heavens door
She is a woman of class, respect, and unimaginable talents
When you read her work you can clearly see her brilliance
When you run across her you will see why people fall in love,
Everything she do, she always take it a step above
So am I'm crazy for falling for a girl like her
Or is the feeling I get believing her love will lift me higher
But I know this good feeling will come to an end
Before anything nice truly began
And a thing called reality decided to step in
And now my life seems like it's in a tail spin
As I began to face my shatter dreams
I now realize she never took notice of me...

The Destination Of Hearts

Trying to figure out where it all began
And back to the moment I first held your hand
The exact point in time your heart met mine
the second I looked into your eyes, my heart unwind
Fearing to awaken into a world with no you
just having a girl like you seems too good to be true
Striving to be that woman you need me to be
Me vowing to be the man of your dreams
Everything I am and will be is because of you
Because, I will never let anything come between us two
You held me accountable for truly being me
You're the reason why my heart is filled and no longer empty
Bringing me up on a standard higher than my own
As I promise that you will never be alone
Forcing me to face my own fears of self destruction
As I protect your heart within the walls of my fortress
Strengthening my weakest moments through embraces
By being the man you dream of everyday
Caring for me in a way that does not shadow my independence
I will give you your space and become your guidance
Perfection is not always found in the words you speak
But, everything I do for you will be special and unique
Yet the purity of your love sets my soul free
And you being the one that makes my life complete
Wondering into horizons never imagined before
But when you get there I will be the one you adore
Finally feeling at one with my past and in love with my present
And the both of us coming together to form a love that is so vibrant
Because at this point I know my future is safe within you
And the bond we now have, nothing will never undo
Just remember this always I want to spend my life with you…

Written: by Richard Lowe &
Monique Jackson

Try

How do you see me
As a modern day Mr. Deeds
How do you like me
As the man of your dreams
Am I your type
Or not worth thinking about twice
Do I have potential
Or anything you find essential
When I call you at home
Are you quick to answer the phone
I think about you all the time
Day dreaming about how to make you mines
Maybe I'm just too simple and shy
And don't have the confidence to catch your eyes
Maybe I'm lacking the right appeal
To have a girl like you head over heels
So before anyone else make you cry
I say you should give us a try.

You

You will always be an Angel in my eye
Because you have proven to me you are meant to be by my side
When I think of you my heart starts to race
You are like the angel God sent my way
You saw things in me, that I didn't see myself
Having you in my life, is the secret to my wealth
I can hear it in your voice, that you really do care
I can tell by your eyes, you will always be there
I can tell by your smile, you mean everything you say
I can tell by your touch, you wish the best for me everyday
I can tell by your kiss, that you love me for my soul
I can tell by your hug, that your love will never get old
Now that you have proved, that you do love me
I promise to make everything in your life complete
The love we share now is like a dream come true
Because everyday I wake up now, I realize that dream is you
As I hold you in my arms and feel your heart beat
I can tell it beats, the letters L-O-V-E
As our love gain strength with every sunrise and sunset
I realize God answered my question and that's why we met
I promise to be the man that you deserve
By you being the one I love, obey, and serve
As I look back now, I should have not let you go in the first place
But I have you back now and I promise to keep that smile on your face
So as I once again stare into those beautiful brown eyes
I promise I will proudly and always be by your side.

You Are

You are everything a woman should be,
you are beautiful, intelligent, sexy, and unique.

You are the hand that comforts me with care, you are
the warmth that insures me when I'm scared.

You are that star I talk to every night, you are that
Angel I pray to have in my life.

You are the desire to my deepest needs, you are that
love that fills my heart when it's empty.

You are that strength that strengthens me when I'm
down, you are that joyful feeling I get when every you
come around.

You are the light, that brighten my days, you are the
woman I think of in every possible way.

You are the woman that parades in my dreams, you are
an angel from heaven sent here to be with me.

You are my treasure my Nubian queen, you are all my
wishes that came to be.

You are the reason I look forward to each day, you are
that beauty I think of in every possible way.

Now that you know all the things that you are, say
you want to be with me and I promise we will go far.

You Never Know

You never know
Who, is watching the things you do
Who, dreams to be with you
Who, wishes to have you by his side
Who, admires that sparkle in your eyes
Who, would do anything to get you close to his heart
Who, understands the woman you are
Who, worships the ground you walk on
Who, prays to be the man you call on
Who, wants to cuddle with you under the stars above
Who, wants to be the only man you love
You never know
How you bring a smile to his face
How you're always on his mind everyday
How he wants you to be his Nubian Queen
How he wants to be the man of your dreams
How he wants to be the burdens of all your pains
How he wants to be that jacket, that covers you in the
rain,
How he wants you to be his sun, his moon, his stars
How he wants you for the woman you are
How he feels you are more than a dream come true
How he can't wait until the day you call him boo.

Your Smile

I wish for a smile
A smile from a girl like you
With an angelic face
And the tantalizing eyes
That I stare at
Begging you to smile more
Because seeing your smile
Is like my sunshine
The first thing I want to see
A thing of beauty
A Kodak moment
Every time I see your face
So when you smile
I just smile back
Because your smile to me is priceless
So perfect that it can't even be dreamed
Because my mind cannot process the beauty of it
Only wish to see it again
So when ever you see me
Just remember to smile
Because it means the world to me.

INSPIRATIONAL

Beautiful Minds

She has a beautiful mind
Like all things that are wasted
Her mind is under appreciated
By a lot of men that take her for granted
Not knowing a beautiful mind is a blessing
Like a gift from the heavens brought before us
A truly sincere and honest person we can trust
A woman that can charm you with just one look
From the sparkles in her eyes
She will let you know things will be alright
As she grabs your hand from your side
You now began to see her beautiful mind
And you start to realize
That she is more than just sexy, and unique
She is intelligent, and everything a woman should be
A woman with class
Whom you can never look past
A strong Nubian black queen
A woman that you only see in dreams
But that is not the only place she is seen
A Beautiful mind is her name
But come correct and don't play games
Treat her with respect and she will do the same
And her love will shower on you like rain
And her love will out last the hands of time
And you will learn just why
Why it is important to get those with a beautiful mind.

Guardians Of The Sea

Through these eyes I see
Being as watchful and alert as I can be
A guardian of the sea
Ready to go save lives
And removed doubts from many minds

Ready to take to the air
The second we get a report a boat launching a flare
Ready to come get you, where many won't dare
We are the guardians of the sea; we will always be there
And by saving your life, is how we prove we care

Quietly patrolling our nations waters
Aiming to shut down, all drug smugglers
Counter narcotic warriors
Like a scary tale, we are their haunters
Not showing fear is our only factor

If you find yourself in the greatest storm in history
Just call for help and we will respond quickly
Remember we are the guardians of the sea
The United States Coast Guard always ready to fulfill our deeds
And proud to call ourselves, Coasties.

Her name is Monique

Her name is Monique
And this is how we came to be
Only things I can say she is like a clone of me
We were two poet's putting our words on myspace
And letting people know if they don't come correct, than don't step our way
We have our ways of getting our points through
And a way of putting our minds together to share our views
I knew she was special I can see it in her eyes
And the way she fabricated her words and rhymes
And told me how much she truly enjoyed mines
She has true beauty and writing skills to match
When I throw out my love line I want her to be my catch
Because her words are truly the best
So yeah I went and put her on my top eight
Because she truly belong in that elite space
So Monique thanks for adding me to your list
Because you have become more than anything I have wish
And one day I hope to seal my thanks with a kiss….

Written: by Richard Lowe
Written: for a truly great friend Monique Jackson

Unknown Level

Not many can run against me when it comes to words
That took a sudden spin the day I met you

Your words reflected upon me and revealed the reality
Mirroring the images of an unknown destiny

Exploring the same life but in different places
Reaching an understanding that the weak can't explain

They know not because they judge too high
Not realizing they bring more material for us to write
Beyond the simplicity they choose to live in

Talk all you want cause you can't touch this
You have to be on this level to see where we going
The only way you reaching here is if we step down and show you....

In dedication to my new friend: Richard Lowe
Written: By Lady Monique

I Am

I am

I am a man

Doing everything I can

A brother who understand

What it means to reach out my hand

To help those that asks for a chance

To get on their feet

To buy food to eat

Their pains…I see

My concerns and help…they need

Like a storming river I rush to their side

To do all I can to take the tears from their eyes

I am

I am the light

That will guide you through life

That brightens your nights

That will make things right

Like the moon in the midnight sky

I will bring you a peace of mind

And you will see why I am one of a kind

By being there time after time

Like a stone wall, I will bear your pains

I will shield you from the rain

I am

I am your conscience

The very source of your functions

I am more than just your thoughts

I am the one, whom points out your faults

When you know you're doing wrong

But I pray you continue to live strong

And remember I'm more than just a man

I am your friend.

I Thank You

I thank you, for all the times I was down
When you came to me and took away my frowns
I thank you, for when I thought all hope was gone
You only insured me that I'm not here alone
I thank you, for the many years I have known you
For some reason when I was in pain, you always knew
I thank you, for all the times you spent listening to me
When I was crying out, how my heart felt empty
I thank you, for all the encouraging advice
And it's you, which I owe with my life
I thank you, for being the friend I can come to
Whenever I felt life was giving me the boot
I thank you in more ways that can ever be said
And I think god every night for having a friend like you, when I go to bed
Thank you Amber for all these great years
For allowing me to move up; instead of down hill
I could not think of anyone that has been there more than you
So I want to say thank you and I love you too.

Written: For Amber Payne a friend for life.

Listen My Sisters

I don't know where I'm going
But I know where I have been
And my Nubian woman
Please listen
To the words I speak
Because I seek
The knowledge
To please your heart
But I seem so far apart
And un in touch
With who you are
Because you chase these men
That hurt you, time and time again
And then grins
When you say how you feel
Because he's the only one playing in your field
But on the real
My ladies
Stop having these babies
By these men, that act like boys
Whose minds seemed annoyed
When you talked about a family
But consequently
He just walks out the door
And says he don't want you anymore
And then you look so surprise
With tears flowing out your eyes
Wondering why
You became a victim to the game
You thought you could make him change
But, who's really to blame

Another single mother
Done wrong by another brother
Who only further
To cause you more hurt
And continue to treat you like dirt
But when you look back
When he was being a mack
And saying how you was all that
The words he used, put a smile on your face
And ask, if he could see you another day
And yes, is the only thing you could say
You were just hooked
Hooked by his good looks
That took
Only five minutes to get your number
So do you sill wonder
Or do you see your blunder
And now you realize
His true intentions, that were disguised
And how your eyes
Lustfully memorized
Allowed you to be blind
But next time
My angelic queens
Men are like books, that you must read
Everything can appear to be cookies and cream
But when you judge a book by it's cover
You will never discover
What some brothers
Really have on their mind
Because love takes time
Because some thing should never be rushed
Because all this sinful lust
Only leads to mistrust

And with out that trust
Relationships are left in the dust
So my sisters, please look before you leap
And make sure you get a real man, that you can keep.

Written: For all the women out there that have been done wrong to.

My Real Friends

This is for all my real friends
The ones who have been there and will be there to the end
My true friends that help me find my way
The ones who always had the right things to say
My true friends I really love all of you
I'm glad that you have always been a person I can come to
For all my friends I have know for all these years
Thank you for helping me when my life was filled with fears
To my friends that I have not known as long
Thank you for giving me a place to belong
My friends I thank you for supporting me and my poetic mind
Thanks for getting to see me for who I am on the inside
When I truly thought all hope was gone
Every last one of you call checking up on me on the phone
My friends I thank you for allowing me to get my life right with God again
And now my friends I can start to repent for all my sins
I thank you for all the smiles you help bring to my face
I thank you for when my mom was sick, how you all prayed
I will never forget how everyone help when life seemed like it out for me
I thank you for not letting me give up on my dreams
My friends, the true back bone in my life that help keep me up
You all are the reason why I'm successful, it has nothing to do with luck
So my friends I just thought I would find a poetic way to say thank you
Because if it was not for you, my life would have been through.

Written: For Sean, Keyon, Tim, Monique, Niyoga, Nicole, Treenice, Cherrie, Tameka, Amber, Larry, Crystal, and LaShunda,

Also to my close friends that are no longer here, I miss you all and love you and I will see you hate heaven gate one day: Pamela, Swanson, Givens, Rhodes, Hemingway, and Doc Rob.

My Sisters

Dear my Nubian queens that have been in my dreams, but lately it just seems, that your souls are in despair, it's like you have lost all hope and no longer car. It's like you have been hurt so long and no one was there, to comforts your pains, to cheer you up when your tears poured like rain, but listen my sister you may not know my name, but I see you crying and sitting alone, wishing to yourself that your pains were gone, and wondering why the man you loved did you so wrong, my sisters what I need you to do is wipe away those tears, because there are men out there that really do care, to break your heart is something they wouldn't dare, but only prove to you they will always be there, my sisters, my beautiful sisters, look at you and your beautiful smile, you have a special persona and unique style, and let me give you a few reason to continue and smile. You live and your learn, not to make the same mistake, you can now make better choices on the men you date, and remember you are the women, things should always go your way, and you not being the toy, the one that gets played.

Poetic Nation

Our words, our poetic minds
Our poetic minds, our flowing rhymes
Our flowing rhymes, that changed with time
That change with time and became well defined

These are our words we express
We express to get off our chest
To get off our chest, to transgress
To transgress, on our poetic quest

A literate warrior armed with nothing more than words
Armed with words and setting our on standards
Setting our standards, with the philosophy of moving forward
Moving forward, to never step backwards

We are writers with a poetic outlook
A poetic outlook, we wrote in a note book
In a note book, where no one would look
Where no one would look until, we have published our first book.

Prayer For A Real Woman

God please bring her on
A real woman
A woman that can free my mind
A woman that loves my soul
Bring her on lord
Let me see her face
Let me gaze into her eyes
I have waited my whole life for her
Please bring her to me
My angel
My equal
My motivation
I'm tired of these sad woman
That don't know what love is
Women that don't remember how Adam treated Eve
Lord I'm ready to love a woman in your name
How you wanted man to love woman
So God before I lose all hope
Please bring her on
Because I have so much love to give
A life time to spend
With the woman you send to me
So God show me my destiny
And Please bring my soul mate on.

Tale Of A Soldier

I am a soldier defending America and it's ways
A protector of freedom, one of many that works night and day
We swore this country we will defend, without thinking twice
Now it seems, it's this country that got us defending our life
We are fighting in a war, that I know we don't belong
And it seems they are telling us, it will be a while before we go home
Are we fighting for America or a mad man in rage
Trying to get the nations of the world to see things his way
We are over here, but our spirit won't die
But why are we over here is the question I keep asking why
I heard the war of terrorism echo a few time through his voice
But invading Iraq was not the right choice
As I sat here many night with tears in my eyes
Because the friends I cared about so much, are no longer by my side
Sometimes we may feel invisible under this armor on our chest
But then we realize under all this, it's just bones and flesh
Now I wonder, did my brothers die in vain
Because to the politicians we are just numbers and not names
They are so quick to go start a war
But the second the draft is mention, they ask what we need that for
We are soldier fighting and dying over lies
And the families of those dying are the ones, that are crying
For every casket that leaves, I say that's another mothers tears
And soldiers like me are beginning to have fears
We are over here and still very much so at war
And mission was never accomplished, so what the hell he say that for
Yes I love my country and I will defend it with my life
But once again I speak the truth, that we are fighting over a lie
So America we call out to you
Vote to bring us home, before more of our lives are through,

Served in the United States Army from Jun 1998- Aug 2004

When I Saw You Cry

When I saw you cry
The tears coming from your eyes
Your feeling no longer in disguise
And your heart crying out why
Wishing you could die
And get away from all these pains
To escape people that play you like game
That leaves your soul feeling like it's restrain
Speeding out of control like a bullet train
And now I see why you act....insane
But I can see you are down
With no real help around
Not one hand to help you off the ground
As you cried more, I will never forget the sound
As it echoed through my soul as I stood in the background
When I saw you cry, I only wanted to whip away yours tears
I wanted to remove all your doubts and fears
I wanted to give you a reason to cheer
I promise to be a true friend for years
And in my eyes you will always be the premiere
I know you feel used
I know you feel so abused
But when I look at you
I know you are in need of a rescue
And I will show you why patience is a virtue
And how your heart should be valued
So let me be the man that put a smile on your face
And whip away all your tears, leaving not a trace
Let me be the dopamine that cures your headaches
And listen as my heart dials the number to your place
Because you are the one, my love wants to embraces.

When A Woman's Heart Cries

For the self proclaim players in life
This is what it sounds like when woman's heart cries
We keep pushing ourselves to do right in life
Hoping to be loved and by someone's side
So come a little closer and stare into my eyes
As I sit here and tell you why
Why hearts cry and chivalry seems dead
Most men just want to get us in bed
And did yawl listen to the words we said
Or were you more focus on getting in our pants
Or picturing me naked in your mind instead
L-O-V-E is what I need
And L-O-V-E is what you never gave me
I just wanted to let you know I would have done anything for you
Just by saying you truly love me too
But, I only found my self being the fool
Where the real men at, where are you my king
I'm a real woman a true Nubian queen
Be my knight and push away my fears
Be my true love and wipe away my tears
Be my inspiration by wanting me in your life
Be all my dreams come true, by making me your wife
I'm a real woman, hear the last of my cries
I know I'm in every man's dream, the woman they want by their side
So hear me, feel me and don't let true love die
Because behind every man, there is a strong woman
Without us, you men don't stand a chance
Learn to love, cherish, and respect our hearts
And I promise nothing! Nothing! Can split us apart.

Who Are We

Who are we? We are heroes, soldiers, the often forgotten ones. A memory of the pass a preexisting thought in most Americans minds. At the peak of any of our nation crisis we are the call to arms, a sleeping giant once again awaken to her battle cries. Fearless forces marching on singing hear us; fear us, for we are American soldiers. A silent warrior, a protector of man, an enforcer of peace.

Who are we? We are the guardians of this great nation. The son's of fallen father's, the leaders of tomorrow. We know the meaning of freedom, for we are the protectors of freedom. We are courageous never yielding to anyone, not even our selves. We are professional at what we do, because we believe in what we do.

Who are we? We are the ones who fight so that Americans can sleep peacefully at night. We are the symbol of freedom and what America is today. We are the souls, that sacrifice it all for this country. We are the sprit of freedom that lives in all Americans. We are the power that gives hope to America's future. We are the stars and strips; the red, white, and blue, that makes you this country's symbol.

Who are we? We are the mighty fist of democracy. Defending truth, justice, and the American way of life. We are the freedom of speech, press, and religion; we are the right to vote and to bare arms; we are America's first and last line of defense. WE ARE AMERICAN SOLDIERS.

You Are The Greatest

You are the greatest
A beautiful lady
An angel of God
Working abroad
Marching in his name
Helping to cure people's pain
To help those in need
That don't have a place to eat
You saw things needed to be reform
By helping to keep the homeless warm
You are one of few, that heard their outcries
I can tell you were determine to help by the looks in your eyes
You are the greatest for what you do
And God had to be showing off when he made you
The things you have done I can't believe
That there are still people out there, helping those in need
An angel to us all, you truly are
Because God bless you with a beautiful heart
Marisa keeping helping those on the streets
And just maybe one day, people like me and you, can end poverty,

Written: For Marisa a girl that I truly admire in so many way; a woman on a level that very few ever reach. Stay bless Marisa, because God is working through you.

Young Lady

She was a beautiful young lady
But lately,
I have been seeing this young lady,
Begging, crying, with
Tears in her eyes,
Looking up at the sky, asking the
Lord why?
Why do they use me and abuse me and leave my soul feeling empty?
I cry to you lord, asking for your help.
For some reason I knew how she felt,
As she dwell her pain away,
Today,
As I sit back in the distance thinking about what to say,
To her, about her pain.
I told her don't feel ashamed,
As I whip her tears away,
Away from her beautiful face,
With no trace,
Of tears running down her face.
She said she came here today to pray,
To get away, from all the things that sadden her day,
She ask for an escape,
An escape from all her pains a sorrow,
I knew than she might see tomorrow,
Because I saw the suicide in her eyes,
As she once again, began to cry,
Asking me why.
She said she was tired of being used,
Used like a carpenter tools, another slot, and a notch on his belt,
Are these, the only men that I'm dealt?
For being a faithful woman to man,
Whose hands only end up in another woman's pants.
I guest....that's a chance you take,
Wait! young lady before you make that mistake,
On saying on how it's your fault that he acts that way,

Listen to what I have to say.
Today I see you beautiful lady, with a sad face,
Wishing all her pains away,
Listen young lady, I know you seek love,
Above all you will find that love,
But in time it will take,
For your heart to find a way,
To a place,
That will erase the sadness from your face,
For you I pray for that day,
When all your pains go way,
For now on don't believe every word that that say
And let them prove their love to you in every possible way,
See young lady in due time you will find that guy,
Who doesn't have lust in his eyes?
And he will see your true beauty that lies inside,
Thank you, I will use my mind
When I'm with guys
To make sure they look past my outside
And see me, for who I am on the inside,
I can't wait until that time,
When I get that guy, that loves me for my mine,
Once gain I say thanks you,
Because if it wasn't for you,
I would have never think twice
About my life,
I owe this night,
To your advice,
My friend until I see you again.

Your Beauty Within

When I look at you, I see more than your unique eyes
I see your sweet personality and your beautiful mind
I see your heart so full of life
I see your soul the bringer of light
A woman like you, so beautiful inside and out
A woman that never leaves people in doubt
You're like an angel; I see it in your smile
You have a unique persona and style
Like a red rose, you are the image of beauty
Your hair can be best describe as jazzy
You are so versatile, in everything you do
I can see why, all men fall in love with you
Everything about you is uncanny
If I was to grade you, you would be a degree
Your charm alone can tame any man
When I'm down, you're the first to lend out your hand
You live this life of excitement and dare you say
And continue to be the woman I dream of everyday
So smile for me, because you brighten my days
And promise me you will never change
You will always come out on top in the end
Because, you have real beauty within.

LIFE

Blind

Is the world going blind
Or is it me that is running out of time
My eyes aren't close, they're open wide
And I can clearly see all this deception in disguised
I wonder is the world at an end
Because some still judge you for the color of your skin
Or simply look you over and not see your beauty within
They speak to you when you're on top, but didn't speak back then
And you now wonder who's out there, that's really your friend
So are they with you for your money or the things they can get
Are they close to you because the person you're with
If you needed money, will they loan it to you and take the risk
If you died,…in their hearts will you be miss
Yes the world is going blind
And changing fast with time
With people not respecting your mind
To me being blind is a crime
Because you truly miss out on things that are truly fine
To those being blind
It's about time
That you open your eyes
And get to know people for their mind.

Chain Reaction-part 1

If I could be born again
In this world without sin
To a place where I have not been
Where my faith is not chosen
Where I can walk these streets in peace
Where I can open up and be me
Like an eagle I'D spread my wings and fly free
And, open my heart for everyone can see
What every word, that comes from my mouth means
Explaining this chain reaction
It's like a follow up to all my actions
The controller of all my functions
I'm now ready to put my ideals in motion
Like a witch and making a potion
And building an unstoppable legion
Who believes in everything I believe in
To fight for a better society
Like candy, crime has its varieties
Our youth, being led so blindly
Committing crimes so violently
Now they're spending life in the pen
Their life gone, before it began!
We could have stop this back than
Before this chain reaction, decided their end...

Chain Reaction-part 2

As we look at these troubled lives
And turn back the hands of time
We start to realize
Deep in the back of our minds
That something that we thought was dead and gone
Something that thousands die for, knowing it was wrong
Something that takes you from everyone you love, feeling all alone
This thing was called slavery
During this time is called the penitentiary
For thousands of our youths, that's all they will see
This is a growing problem that we all must agree
By fighting to keep them from becoming history
Let's alter this negative chain reaction
By fighting it with love and positive actions
Which results, can be forever lasting
So hear my voice fathers
Feel my strength mothers
Seek my knowledge brothers
And love again my sisters
Come together with love and fight
Because I don't want to see this chain reaction, take another life
I never want to see another mother or father cry
I never want to see people asking the Lord why
With true love, we can conquered all
So relax and stay calm, like rain fall
And change this chain reaction and its forsaken ways
To more constructive and positive days.

Change

Want to know about the real front line
Where you got to many brothers shooting and dying
That leaves mothers and fathers screaming and crying
With their sons now gone and many asking why
Not knowing how they lived their troubled lives
So let's began the real stories from the front line
It's like a war zone out here in these streets
You see it on the news every time you turn on your TV
It's not fear factor, its real reality
Where people has to hustle just for their kids can eat
With many forgetting this is real poverty
Right here in America in all our city streets
So how much longer should this carnage go o
How much longer should the poor be left alone,
Or is something that is ignored until they are dead and gone
The problem is only going to get bigger and cross your side of the tracks
And than it's going to be you watching your back
And honestly we both know we don't want that
So let's sit back and think on how to make things better
And find a way that all our minds can come together
And whether away all this suffering forever
So come together right now before me
And let's put an end to this thing called poverty
Let's stump out violence on our city streets
Let's flush out the dealers to make our community's drug free
Let's encourage our young kids to pick up and book and read
And they will learn that knowledge is life's key
Let's stop degrading our women and start treating them like queens
Because they are our mothers, sisters, lovers, and the angel in our dreams
Let's love and show respect for our fellow man
And on this day, let's make this change began.

Dear God

Dear God I know it's been a while since we spoke
And I found myself taking your powers as a joke
But God I have been going through so much
And waiting patiently waiting for your gifted touch
I lost faith God and turned my back on you
But since I have lost my faith, my life seems like it's through
God I am saved and even had place for you in my heart
But since I went to Iraq, it seemed we have drifted apart
I want to know why you allowed so much suffering and pain
I want to know why so many kids have died in vain
I want to know what happen to the love
I wonder when I prayed to you were you listening from above
I've been a soldier for this country why can't I be one for you
I want you to accept me back into your life and love me too
I want these burdens off me to be a better man
So I can continue to help people the best way I can
I want the power of you Lord back in my life
Because I've done you wrong and now I want to make things right
God I know you have someway touched us all
And God when ever I need help you will be the first I call
I end this letter to you God and hope you hear my cries
And I pray you are willing to be back by my side.

To The only person that have always been there for me I'm sorry God

Each Others Dreams

I feel you, but do you feel me
Because right now it just seems
They we both share the same dream
The dream of be loved
We dream to be held and hug
By a person the was sent from the man above
I look at you and feel your desires
I feel what your heart admires
Maybe I'm lost in your near perfect beauty
And saying to myself I really wish you knew me
Because I would love to get the chance
The chance to hold your hand
To be your man
To do all I can
To keep
To keep....
That smile on your face
And never erase
True happiness from your life
Because women like you should never ask why
You don't have a real man by your side
I wish to look you in you eyes
And tell you how happy you make me
Because I feel we are each others most wanted dreams.

I Will

For you I will
For thy heart I will fulfill
For thy love
I will be the one you hug
For thy smile
I will do all I can to make your dreams worthwhile
For thy heart
I will charm it like thy melody tunes from Mozart
For thy love
I will treat you like a true angel from above
For thy kiss
I will honor you like a Nubian princess
For thy happiness
I will do things for you that are priceless
For thy to be in my life
I will make you the addiction that gets me high
Like a kite flying high in the sky
I will began and end each day with you on my mind
Like that of a sunset and a sunrise
I live to see the beauty in your eyes
I want to be the one you embrace
When it comes to you there are a thousand words I can say
I just want you to be the one I love, honor, and obey.

Four Season

It's like 90 degrees as I feel the warm breeze, pass right through me. I look to the sky and take advantage of the sunshine as I sit here laying in the sand with a water bottle in my right hand, trying to stay cool in this heat, that beats down on me. The sound of those waves, oh those waves, that gets me high like I just left a rave, I can taste the salt in the air during the best times of the year......I now find myself without my warm breeze and I notice the trees are starting to lose their green leaves, but the trees are still a thing of beauty, that I think all people should see, these autumn colors so beautiful and bright, I think God for blessing me for seeing things like this in my life and during these moments the weather is not to warm or cold, but just right. I watch the kids has they laughed and played, in a pile of leaves that someone just raked....Those leaves are now all gone as I sit here in this freezing cold, that got me shivering in my bones, everything seems to be gone all around, just a hard cold feeling I get when I place my hand on the ground, but it doesn't rain anymore, just snows ,...the very thing most people adore, the white sleek ice, that people everywhere want to grab and slide and take that a ride down the steepest hills, seeking the ultimate thrills, to fulfill there adrenaline fuel minds, but it's now time for the snow to melt away and lots of showers, that bring flowers in May. Things are turning green again and no longer gray and the kids grab there kites and run to the fields to play. People are at the beach again and looking for volleyball games to play in, You can here the sound of bats being cracked reminding you baseball is almost back and let's not for get about the ones taking a break from school, doing crazy thing to see who is the biggest fool, with everyone enjoying life without any fears, because these four changes each happen once a year. Summer, Fall, Winter, and Spring, these are the four seasons and their names.

Just A Thought

Just a thought
Of a perfect world
Free of disease
Free of poverty
Filled with laugher
Showered in love
Just a thought
That men got along as one
That money was not the plague of man
People not dying over drugs
Women not selling themselves on the streets
Politicians not being deceitful
Just a thought
That there were no more wars
No more crying mothers
No more lost brothers
No suddenly made widows
That there was peace among earth
Just a thought
If all this was true
That I thought in my head
That I wish was true
That I wish I had the power to make happen
Then this would be a perfect world
Instead of this reality call life.

Look At Us Now

Look at us now
Black and proud
Talking loud
Hopeless dreams
Self proclaim kings
All this hate
Too many fakes
Look at our faces
No respect
What the heck
We are a mess
Single mothers
Looked up brothers
We got to move further
Leave the drugs
Change the thugs
Learn to hug
We got to make it through
Without love, help is few
Learn to pray to you know who
Look at us now
We got to make that change
Stop taking life as a game
Learn your brothers name
Life is getting harder
We got to be smarter
And men be a father
To what you help make
For your child sake
Who wants your grace
We got to move on

Stop doing each other wrong
And join together to be strong
Just think about all the times
We have been deny
Always criticize
Taking as a joke
Thought of as being broke
And hooked on dope,
But we got to show them all
That blacks will no longer fall
But only stand tall
With our heads held high
Marching side by side
Looking everyone one in the eyes
So look at us now
Look around
And you will see
That God is here for you and me

Written: For all my brothers and sisters out there, even if you don't like me I still love you. I still believe that this world can change for the better. Just some people will take longer to open their eyes. God is good, he will find a way for you. He did for me.

Mother, Father

Father please for give her for she does not know what she do
And she may be the reason why I never met you
You leaving me long before I was two
So growing up, knowing who my father is, I never had clue
So father where ever you may be
I just want to know why you never tried to find me
But right now it just seems
That I grew up alone
Because father while your still gone
Mother started drinking and doing us so wrong
And leaving my brother and me in a empty home
She started drinking more and got on drugs over a man
A man who was no better then the crap you put in a trash can
And sadly in 2001 mother's life came to an end
A close to her chapter before it really began
Mother listen to what I'm about to do
Because I will never be like you
Falling for those lame lines like you use to
I'm all grown up now and I still got a lot of learning to do
And all that sweet talk crap I don't listen to
There is only one promise that I can keep
I'm going to take care of my brother and me
I'm not going to be another female selling herself on the streets
I'm never going to let a man put his hands on me
I'm never going turn my back on the one's I love
But prove to them I got their backs when push comes to shove
See I am proud of myself and all the good things I have done
I am proud to say no man will ever have me on the run
I went from a hurt little girl
To a woman who runs her own world
So look into my eyes and yawl will see

That I'm doing every thing to make yawl proud of me
  I just wish we could have been a happy family
  Instead of the mother and father that left me.

My Puzzled Life

I was once a complete puzzle, showing the image of who I was
Many pieces, put together like the patterns on a rug
But my puzzle was shattered all over the place
And I began feeling like my life is in displace
Like a lost soul wondering about in a dwell
In a hot a morbid place, that closely resembles hell
When my puzzle was shattered I started losing my way
And it seems nothing that I did allowed me any leeway
Before I can have that happiness of freedom, that my soul desires
I need to get right with God and do as he requires
Because my faith, is what will guide me through this hardship
Because all my once big problem, now appears as a blip
With my puzzle almost back to the way it us to be
I now make things happen, that I use to only dream
With only a few pieces left, I'm almost complete
And I have learned, that only God himself can judge me
With my pieces back together with me moving forward
I have only one person to think and that is you Lord.

Poverty

We have spent billions in the war in Iraq
They wish food could have been bought with that
We tend, not to eat all the food on our plates
They wish they had something that could take their hunger away
We complain about a ticket we got issued
They die, because they don't have any food
We tend to get off of work to go hit the streets
They listen for United Nations planes, hoping to get food to eat
We have a home and a roof over our heads
They have nothing and the hard dry ground is their bed
We have cars and planes to take us where we want to be
They don't even have shoes, to put on their feet
When it comes to the suffering in Africa we pretend not to see
The dying and suffering from this thing called poverty.

Untitled

I sit back
And relax
And pretend
Not to see
All these kids
On the streets
Smoking weed
Getting high
Killing time
Wasting their lives
And committing crimes
Pulling guns
Thinking its fun
To have people on the run
All these gangs
Acting insane
Killing over a name
It's time for a change.

We Pray For A Change

We pray for a change
A change for the kids and their families, who don't have thing
Whose lives were change
When a hurricane
By the name
Of Katrina came their way
Blowing and howling as it came ashore that day
Only thing they could do is hold on to something and pray
Wondering in fear, if staying there was a mistake
Katrina has pass with devastation and turmoil in her wake
The country left in shock with very little to say
A city now flooded by two levy breaks
And thousands still wondering will they see the next day
"We call to our government" as they cried with plead
"Help us save us from this misery
Because we are dying from hunger and disease"
Mr. President, don't you see our sadness or just the color of our skin
And is that the reason why it took so long for help to begin?

What Can I Do

What can I do
In a world that seems doomed
When people in government have it out for you
And they talk down like you don't have a clue
But I know more than what people think
I just take in a lot and let it sink in
Because I can sense the end
To a nation filled with hate
And you hear about kids being raped
Or innocent lives being taken
Or a baby being shaken
Or another family forced into the streets
A lot of people wonder how can this be
All this turmoil in the land at the free
And millions dying from these sexually transmitted diseases
We can clearly see the signs
But yet we are wasting time
Because it doesn't affect our lives
But deep in my mind
I realize
That this world is due for a change in its ways
But it seems I'm the only one who believes he can save the day
I'm only one person, who will listen to what I say
So I guess we all must just pray
So as I look out for every last one of you
While our world and way of life continues to be doomed
Just remember I'm one man, what can I do.

PAIN

How Long Should You Love

How long should you love
After your heart feels like it' been swept under a rug
Do you keep giving in to the sad lies
Hoping there is a good reason to stay by their side
Do it seems that your love was just a loan
Because they only did your heart wrong
Do you feel no one else could want you
Because all of the stuff that they put you through
Do you wonder why they did you that way
And when they say I love you, do they mean what they say
Do you wonder why you have tears in your eyes
But, when you look at them, their eyes remain dry
See love was meant for two
And you can't love someone that don't truly love you
Remember if they love you as they say
They will show you how…everyday.

Lost Of Love

I had something so beautiful and pure once
A woman that had me day dreaming plenty of nights
Constantly on my mind
Her angelic ways
Her memorizing eyes and smile
Her charm, that had me charmed
Our intimate moments we shared
The times I taste her over and over
I can still feel the wetness from her
I truly had what I wanted
A real woman, selected by God
A women that was always there for me
But some where, I turned her away
And as time past she disappeared what seemed to be forever
A woman like that gone
The woman of my dreams gone
But my heart continues to beat for her
Hoping to hold her again
Hoping to look into her eyes
Hoping to ask her to forgive me
For what ever I may have done
This who is who I am
I believe you don't just say I love you
But show your love to the one you love
To value her
Like God attend Adam to value eve
To cherish her
Like you cherish the air you breathe
To love her
Like you would like your soul to be loved
But I come to realization of life

And realize that I had my chance with this angel
And if she was truly my soul mate
She would be right here in my arms right now
With her smile and love
Melting away at my heart
But I must not dwell on the past
The moments in my life
Where happiness dominated my life
When I felt, I meant something to someone
I will hold noting back
But I love you, but I can't hope any more
For us to become one again
Because it takes two to love
You know I love you so much
And you will always be a part of my world
But I got to find someone that is special like you
I know you are reading this
And I hope no one ever hurts you again
Because a strong Nubian woman like you
Deserves only true love in your life
Because I made mistakes in the years
But my tears will be happy tears to see you smile again
Bye my first true love….
And no longer again will I have the lost of love.

Love hurts

Love hurts a dwelling and relentless pain from the inside
That leaves your heart feeling like it's been freeze-dried
Love is the emotion that seems to shut your life down
Like your life's reactor, is having a meltdown
But the lost of love is the reason why your heart cries
Your broken heart is the reason why, you wish you could die
Your many tears that formed from these pains and sorrows
Crying yourself to sleep hoping these pains will be gone tomorrow
This endless fight that is tearing you apart on the inside
Punishing your heart over and over, like it has been founded guilty of a crime
The love you give to others appears to be just a loan
I now know you're crying,... saying your heart is better left alone
You resent the person that got you feeling this way
And you open your eyes and realize there is a thin line between love and hate
The next time you put your heart out there, just be alert
Because we all know how much love can really hurt.

Love Lost

Who knows
The roads
Love will take you
The pain it will put you through
The hopeless reality that pulls you in
That tears you apart within
That got you on a emotional rollercoaster
Praying for these feeling to be over
Like a disturbed mind
With crying eyes
You dwell on the pain
Boarder line insane
With the powerful feeling
That's quickly
Tearing you apart
And leaving a emotion mark
That you will never forget
Because this....
Feeling in you life
Will have you thinking twice
About getting close again
Because that feeling will never end
And your can never really recover
From the lost love on another.

My Brother's Soul

My brother you will be missed in this life
because the person I am today you're the reason why
Like a true friend should, you always stuck by my side
And you reminded me to always look a man in the eye
Now it seems like a different world with you gone
And doing the things we use to, seems so wrong
I know nothing can change the fact that you're gone
I will always keep you in heart and soul
Remember a person by the way they lived is what I was told
You were my brother's soul my very best friend to the end
We both vowed this country we will defend
Because the love we have for our country they won't understand
We were more then just soldiers; we were warriors at heart
Whoever would have thought that one bullet could split us apart
You just got caught between two guys and their mess
And the next thing you know you're bleeding from the chest
And in that parking lot your soul would finally rest
I attended your ceremony with sorrow in the air
Saying to myself I'm sorry when you got shot that I was not there
This just doesn't seem fair, a man like you just gone
Leaving a precious little girl all alone
And I pray you find heaven because that's your new home
I will keep a good eye on your family
Because I know you would do the same for me
Since your death my life seems cold
But you will always be remembered as my brother's soul.

Written: with Stanley Swanson in mind

Sad Little Boy

I'm about to tell you all story filled with sorrow and pain

About a hurt little boy, for now I will leave out is name

All the kids picked at the way he looked and dress

This little boy couldn't help,.. that he looked a hot mess

Because he grew up poor and his mom always did her best

This little boy would always put his head down in class

And glance up every once in a while to see how much time has pasted

He wasn't worried about what he got on his grades

Because he was to scared to speak up, if he had something to say

He would leave school early before all the kids would get out

Because the kids, when they saw him, they never had anything positive to talk about

But this young kid problems did not end in school

Because he had to go home to a drunken fool

This sad little boy hated the way he feels

And he ran to the bathroom and quickly swallowed down 80 aspirin pills

He clean up his moms house and went to his bed room,

Laying on his bed hoping he would die soon

The next thing he knew the paramedics were at the door

And his sister yelled out "help my brother, because he don't want to live no more"

The doctor came up him and said drink down this charcoal right away

Because trust me son you wouldn't like the other way

The mother of this boy, decided to get him some help

Because she never knew what pains, her son really felt

The little boy stood and said his name to the group

And told them all why he wished his life was through

The boy said, I can't help the way I look, God made me this way

And how come when I was in tears they continue to pick at me anyway

The little boy grew up and now he is in high school

And he met the first girl who he would say I love you to

This girl took up for him till the very end

Because sadly she kill herself after she was rap by her guardian

He hurt so much that not a tear came from his eyes
He just crawled to a corner and asked God why
Why the only person who ever took up for me is gone
And now I'm once again in this harsh world alone
I know this is a sad story and hard to believe
But the little boy it talks about is…..me.

People watch what you say, because you never know how much, that stuff really hurts.

Suicide

I'm losing it; I think I'm going crazy
Brintelzya I'm going to miss you baby
But it just seems lately
That my mind is so confused
And a thousand things telling me what to do
Take your life
End it with this knife
And I than began asking these voices why
Why they feel I deserved to die
The said you're weak now Richard you're not the man you use to be
You are what a blind man sees
Nothing!!
Like a small fish in the sea
People never appreciated the things you did
Women never love you for your heart within
And every girl, you asked out told you no… over and over again
See your weak Richard, but I know it's not your fault
Because for some reason you believe loved can be bought
Only heart break and defeat is the only thing you caught
No one cares about you and your pains
No ones is here to extinguish your flames
See people only took your life as a game
Because you were Mr. Nice Guy always going out your way
To only have a girl tell you to get out her face
See Richard we know you dreaded each day
So as you listen to the voices in your head
Just think about it, your better off if your dead
You won't be miss
You're not someone that is cherish
So grab that knife
And end your life

There you go put it to your wrist
And cut your veins until you see a blood mist
And slowly die as your body falls to the floor
And lay there until your heart beats no more
Tears began to enter my eyes
I'm now scared to death of my thoughts of suicide
And I said to God as I look to the sky
This can't be the way I feel, because I don't want to die
Give me the strength to bear my burdens
Because I want to live and I do know not that for certain
So free me from these suicidal thoughts in my head
Because I don't believe nothing these voices said
So now I lay me down to sleep
I pray to you lord my soul to keep
And if I shall die before I wake
I pray to you lord my soul to take.

Sometimes life gets hard and you have crazy thoughts.

The Loan Of Love

I thought I knew you, but I guest I was wrong
Because this whole time, my love was a loan
My tears from you has multiplied
And now I wonder who really was the person I allowed by my side
Everything about you to this point has been a lie
Like a person at a masquerade ball in disguised
You told me all these things you like about me
But I know you are full of crap and that I can clearly see
I would have done anything for you to keep that smile on your face
But since I have came to my senses, I realize I was the one being played
I can't believe I wasted all this time with you
You knew from the beginning that it wouldn't be just us two
Care, trust, and love are words you should never speak
Because you are the one that was so determine to go cheat
Yes I'm bitter now and glad you're gone
Just makes me sick now, knowing my love for you was a loan
The next time you take a look at yourself,
Just remember you are the one that needs help
I'm going to move on and keep being me
And I'm glad I'm rid of you, because you are like a disease
I'm going to cut these chains that attaches me to you
And let you know for sure, that we are through….

This Is How We Say Good Bye

This is how we say good bye
With anger in our eyes
Like two dragons going at it
In a violent fiery pit
With no feeling held in
Like we knew it was the end
To a friendship that meant so much to me
All the hate with us I can't believe
It's breaking my heart to say good bye
I thought we were friends for life
I can not believe how much this hurt
But I made every effort
To save the animosity between us
But we both lack that trust
Why did we have to say good bye
It's like I want to cry
Tell me is this really fair
For both of us to act like we don't care
I dial your cell phone
But all I get is another busy tone
I wish I had the power to edit life
I would hit rewind and make things right
We should have never said good bye
I keeping asking my self why
How did I lose someone as special as you
You got rid of me like a twenty four hour flu
It seem like destiny was about to began
But I guest that destiny was really our end
I'm just so damn confuse
Honestly what did I do to you
I can tell you are in distress

And I only want you to have the best
But I guest that's how it goes
Your true feeling for me expose
But you should have saw the look in my eye
That I never wanted to say good bye.

UNDERSTANDING ME

Believe In Me

Excuse me
Can you tell me why it's so hot
Why does it feels like my life came to a stop
I'm stuck in a point I don't want to be in
It's like I'm being punish early for my sins
It's starting to break me down
And I'm reaching out, but there are no friends around
Either I'm losing my way or I have completely lost it
When it comes to trials and tribulations, I'm first to get pick
I'm scared now and I don't want to go ahead
I'm at all stop now, like a boat in the water…dead
I can't even began to see myself anymore
It's like I'm not moving and being stepped on like a mat at a door
It's like my mind and soul is in a world that don't exist
And I feel like I'm falling deep into a abyss
If I can find the energy to believe again
To have that energy that motivated me back then
Then just maybe my life will be at peace
My mind finally at ease
But first of all, I got to once again believe in me.

Daddy's Home

Bri, I love you do much girl, and I want you to know you will always be my world, like diamonds and pearls, you are priceless to me the only person my heart envies, you're like the stars in my skies, you're the sparkle in my eyes, you're the reason I fight to survive. Baby it seems that daddy is gone, but all you have to do is pick up a phone, daddy will be there, you will never be alone, when I pick up the phone and hear your voice I will just stand there with a smile and rejoice as I listen to your laughter and joy. Thinking how lucky I am to have a little girl like you, who learned to do so much by the age of two and I want you to know all things you've done I'm proud of you too, like you dancing around singing your ABC's or giving me a hug and saying how much you love me. Bri I love you so much baby, my little lady and if anyone hurts you daddy will go crazy. How could you blame me, because every time I look into your eyes I see my own side and I will never let my love pass you by. Baby I know it seems wrong with daddy gone but, remember my love will continue on.

Written: For Brintelzya, my little angel.

From, Through, And To

Through these eyes, I see
Through my mind, I dream
Through life's challenge I face
From darkness comes day
Through my hopes, I wish
From the beginning, I plan to finish
From my sorrows, comes relief
From my triumphs, comes defeat
Life is either a lost or a win
What begins, comes to an end
What was once lost, is now founded
What goes up comes down
A hug is followed by a kiss
And first times are always cherished
Through my religious faith
I find a way to make I through each day
From the family, I love
To the angel, that watch us from above
To my special little girl
For the reason, I will give her the world
To life, that I feel is no longer a test
To my burdens, that are finally off my chest
To my soul mate, that I have yet to meet
To God for blessing me.

I Am A Man

I know who I am, a man
Do you
You are still walking in shallows
I'm making them
My life is like clock work
I rise and set like the sun
I don't need to be heard
Because, I'm making my way
No one can hit me harder the life
So, no person will ever get me down
I no longer dream
Because what I desired most I now have
I am who I am, a man
I'm not living a lie
I am real black man
Not some stereotype of a black man
I push my self harder every day
To be better than what I was yesterday
I don't fear tomorrow
I welcome it with open arms
My strengths, lies in my heart
What ever you do to me
I just take it in and spit it out in words
I see no limits in my abilities
And no weakness in my beliefs
My only fear is failure
And my goals is to always move forwards
And always have my own identity
Not some fabricated black man that you see on TV
I am who I am, a man
Because I am a man of my own.

I Walk Alone

I walk alone
When all my friends are gone
I walk alone in life
Pushing myself to the max to do right
I walk alone with my heart shattered
Trying to recover from my soul being battered
I walk alone with fire in my eyes
Questioning a lot of things, asking myself why
I walk alone listening to everything people say
And time after time I prove them wrong everyday
I walk alone for miles facing me fears
Not giving up, even after my eyes are filled with tears
I walk alone not knowing what's to come
But, I promise I will not stop, until all my goals are done.

I'm Done

I can write a thousand poems on how to treat a lady,
But trust me this will not be vaguely
Just very direct and precise
I like a guided missile ready to take a flight
I know about you being shallow and vain
So now it's time for my emotions to be unchained
To let you know I don't like the way you did me
And I'm now seeing clear and no longer blurry
So you want a good man, I heard that cry before
I heard it so much I'm going to name that line encore
You really don't want a good man like me
You want one you can show off to your friends like a trophy
And the second he played you, you got tears running out your eyes
But you knew it was coming so don't look so damn surprised
Want me to talk about something very deep
Like how he knocks you up and then leave
And than your kids grow up calling another man daddy
And you got to work three jobs just to make it weekly
But who am I to chastise on how you live your life
Because I am formally know as the nice guy
Over the years you proved you never cared
And you're the reason why my soul is in despair
So I hope you had fun playing my emotions like a game
I know you did because you're a playa as you proclaim
So can I end this with some words in my behalf
Because in due time I will have the last laugh.

Mayhem Undone

I'm on the verge of losing my mind
It's like I'm slowly dying with time
It's like I'm been suffocated
By a drug that's leaving me so sedated
I really need to find myself
I'm like an unlabeled book on the shelf
I'm wondering does happiness really matter
Because it only leads to my heart being shattered
I'm really losing control of my life
You can see the fears as you stare into my eyes
I got to give this thing call love a break
Because I really hate feeling this way
Sometimes I don't know who to trust
But keeping my enemies close is a must
I really need to get my life back together
And start making things better
I admit I have made mistake
In a lot of choices I have made
It's now time for me to be accountable for them
Because it's time to end the mayhem.

Me

Is it me or can anybody see. The faults I have on the inside…the constant worry on my mind. The construction of backwards functions, that leads to my destruction. It's like my great walls, the ones that have protected me will fall…and after all,…the dust has settle…I lay there like a rose peddle, without my feet on the ground…thinking how can I let things get me down. I got to first love myself, before I love another, I got to find the man in me before I go any further,. I got to face my fears….and wipe away my tears. I got to learn to be the man I use to be, …powerful and strong and keep in mind,…my destiny is where I belong, to be successful and never look back, moving forward…now that's where I'm at. A proud black man, that is more than determine, to do right in life, not throwing the dice and looking a life as a gamble……but make everything that I do an example of what a real man is suppose to be, strong, intelligent, respectable, and loving…that's me.

My Demons

My troubled dreams that I see when I sleep
Are life's demons taking control of me
I would take hard angry swings at it
But how can I hit something when I can't see through the mist
It's grabbing me and taking control of my life
I'm begging and pleading, but it does not hear my cries
The pure strength of this demon, I can not believe
As it holds me off the ground and drains the life from me
Look here demon you have been controlling me for years
Bringing trials, tribulations, and many painful tears
Now you are trying to take my soul, which I cherish,
But, look here demon! You can not have it!
This is my soul, my life, and my dreams
And I will not let you take those from me
The demon yelled and dropped me to the floor
And said your soul is strong again and I don't want you anymore
I was now able to see through the mist and could not believe what I see
This demon I was fighting the whole time…was me.

EVO

My name is Evo, I am like no other
I educate my mind, so that life can take further
I am not a fad follower, trying to be in the in crowd
Because, the man I am, makes me feel proud
I have changed with time, but continue to keep it real
I continue to move up, instead of down hill
My words are the image of what's on my mind
The way I act, are my words defined
I'm old school and new mixed into one
I live strong and constantly seeking wisdom
I call myself Evo, because I have evolved
I'm ready to face all challenges, until they are solved
I'm going fight for a dream, that an Icon once had
Instead of wondering about like an nomad
My only goal is to make this world a better place
By helping those whom minds are displace
Like a renegade, I will do it alone
Defending my cause, like an evzone
I am Evo, hear my words
If you're about hurting people, than consider me a hazard.

Not Giving a Chance

Hi my name is Richard
I'm the nice guy
That's always pushed to the side
That is always there
To give his hand
That hear all your cries
It's breaking me down
To see how I'm been used
How I'm being taken for granted
This constant judge of my character
This miss use of my kindness
Got me feeling so frantic
You all claim you want a man
That can get in a mans place
That's truly faithful to you
The romantic type
A real family man
Who sticks to you like glue
But can yawl really hear me
When I say I can be that man
All the man your heart desires
That pleases your mind, body, and soul
But I guest the looks are required
I can tell yawl have been afraid
To have a real man
And I see now I was the fool
To ever think anyone would give me a chance.

One Day

One day my smile will not be fake

One day a man will stand behind his handshake

One day I will be respected for who I am

One day more than just me will give a damn

One day a woman will show me true love

One day I will brighten days like the sun above

One day I will not be judge off looks

One day people will read about me in books

One day I will have the girl of my dreams

One day "moving forward" will be more then my theme

One day I will touch thousand of lives

One day I will answer all of those who cry

One day the world will know my name

Because one day!. One day! I will make a change.

One Voice

With my one voice
I will march alone
And stand in the place of those who can't stand
To be the fist for those who can't defend themselves
To be the courage for those who have fears
With my one voice
I will find ways to help the poor
Help young teens off the streets
To give hope to where it was lost
To give love to where it is needed
With my one voice
I will help eradicate poverty
I will be a role model to those who look up to me
I will be the echo of freedom heard around the world
I will be the hand that pulls people out of holes
With my one voice
I will encourage people to do right
I will end black on black violence
I will give people a reason to dream again
I will show that all men are equal
This all can happen in my one voice
If heard by many and echoed by many.

One person can't change the world, but when you hear someone trying to help others, hear their ideals and join hands to help make this a better world. Where poverty, racism, violence, and poor health care, don't exist.

Reborn

Have you ever thought about the day you were born
And from than to now how your life seemed torn
This is how I was reborn
There are a thousand things that I could say
To get people to see things my way
As I sit here driving myself insane
From all these emotion and pains
That has a hold of me like steel chains
As I feel this anger flowing through my veins
Making me feel more and more derange
But these pains!
I can not get of my mind
As I spend hours asking myself why
Why does it seem like my life is on the dark side
Kept in a corner and push aside
As tears began to enter my eyes
And I beg out to an empty space with my cries
As I feel my soul slowly dying
With every single breath I breathe
I began to fall to my knees
And my mind began to see
All the tribulations that have happen to me
Tribulations that are killing me like a rare disease
If I could just find a way
To put my life back in place
And erase
This stress that burden me today
I just reach out my hand in this open space
Hoping some one would look up and notice
Me franticly reaching out my hand
And just when I thought I was at the end

I was grab and grab hard by a friend
Who told me I was not in dreamland
And there is nothing they won't understand
I am your friend and now I demand
Why you didn't come to me in the first place
Why you waited until you feel this way
Why I must find you down and out like this today
You're my friend and I'm going to put your life back in place
You just have to be man and be strong
And still be happy for all your friends that are gone
Just because they're gone, you're not alone
Why can't you see
That we all need you here indeed
At that moment my heart felt no longer empty
And I starting feeling this energy
That flowed motivation all the way through me,
And I jump to my feet
Not being able to believe
That I was healed from that painful disease
That left me so depressed and stressed
I so glad to have that off my chest
I feel like a new man
In this new life I will began
And I owe it all to a friend
Who healed me when my life was torn
And now I will be reborn.

Say This Once

I'm just going to say this once
Don't mistake me for a punk
Don't take my kindness for weakness
Because I can become very heartless
Like the weather I can change
Bringing lighting and rain
My words are brutal
And my soul is ready to rumble
I will yield to no man
I'm in my own jungle, like Tarzan
My strength is what got me this far
My senses are keen, like that of a jaguar
So if you think you know me, than think again
Because, I'm the best there is, like the hit man
I hope you understood everything you just read
Because this is the new me, the old one is dead.

Thinking

I sit here
Almost mindless
Rethinking things in my head
Rethinking the dumb things I did
When I almost beg a girl to be with me
And now I'm really thinking
And displacing
All my thoughts
Trying to truly find
Find what I really want
Because my riches I never flaunt
Never showing
Just how deep my pockets really are
Because I now understand these women
Thinking just because what's between their legs
They can just get me to do whatever
I don't give, ...to get something in return
I give,... from my heart
These girls keep looking down on me
But the truth is, the truth is
They don't know about me
Because if they did
They would know I just don't look at the horizon
I walk past it
I just don't say I will
I do it..
Because if you ever feel you can judge me
Then you just do it
Because in my mind
I know where I'm going
And I rather be turned down, by a million woman
Then waste my time with a million fake ones.

Untitled 12-03-06

I just thought you should know
As I continue to walk this road
The things that are on my mind
Trying to out run time
Trying to prevent an end
Before anything really began
I wonder do I make the right choices
Or should I have listen to the voices
It's like life is taking shots at me
And promising me, it will show no mercy
I will never be loved by those I care for
Just looked down on , like dirt on the floor
I'm not perfect and will never be
But will someone say why, no one wants me
I have walk alone for all these years
With no one to help me with my fears
So I call out to anyone out there
Hear me and show me you care.

What I Am

What I am
I am nothing more than a man
And I am more than what I seem
I am a soldier that fought in the sandy desert of Iraq
I am the not the corrupt politicians that put me there
I am a protector of all people
I am not a bigot, rapist, or murder
I am a believer of all people
I am not a racist that think all races are obsolete
I am the all Seeing Eye
I am not a mindless unaware person
I am loyalty
I am not betrayal or mistrust
I am honor
I am not pride less or a disgrace
I am self-less service
I am not an egomaniacal dictator
I am a father
I am not the dead beaks that disowns their spawns
I am a brother
I am not the one that will bring disgrace to my family
I am a true friend
I am not the one who encourages you to do wrong
I am a listener
I am not the type to go tell your business
I am further more your sun shining bright
The moon in your sky
The hope to your prayers
The love that shows I care
I am!
I am!!
I am!!!........
Just me.

Why Should I

Why should I lend my hand
To those who don't give a damn
Why should I shed my tears
For those who only cause them
Why should I keep going out of my way
For those that wouldn't do it for me
Why I should give respect
When other never do
Why should I be kind
When it is taken for weakness
Why should I care
When no one else does
Why should I give my last dime
For anyone who wouldn't give up theirs
Why should I keep being the nice guy
Just to finish last
Why should I care about single mothers
I will never be one
Why should I care about drugs
I don't sell or use them
Why should I care about poverty
When no ones else does
Why should I care is a woman is called out of her name
When she allows it to happen
Why should I really care about anything bad in the world
When people don't care about me.

LAST WORDS

Behind My Words

I write because behind my words, lies a man in pain, that only wishes to be truly loved...for love is the key to my life and until I have found that, I just dwell in a space with no walls or sides, just free falling to no where. My tears are no longer wet just dry, my heart no longer beat for passion, but just beat for me to smile. I'm at a point where I only wish that life can just take me now and free me for this hell, that is like a prison to me, each time I walk out my door, is like hours in the box in the yard. I don't know if I'm pushing myself to much, like I was cramming for a test. Maybe when I look at life and myself, it's not life that is knocking me down, it's me, being to hard on myself. Never letting up and just putting myself down and not given myself enough credit. So behind my words speak of moments in my life, the good or the bad. So by reading my poems you read points in my life where I express my emotion through a pen to put you in my shoes, to allow you to feel pain, and just maybe you will see why I shed tears or why I smile. So I welcome everyone to my world the world of Evo meaning evolution, because I feel I have evolved into something more and better then what I can ever expected and with that being said I am happy with my life and thank God for everything.

I Write

I'm going to write
Until I die
To ease my mind
Every time
The mood hit's me
The words I speak
Yawl can't believe
The words you see
So much sorrow and pain
Richard is my name
I'm still the same
Ain't nothing change
But I'm going to keep on writing
I've face my fears
I've cried many tears
Over these painful years
But guest what I'm still here
I've done my crimes
And served my time
Now I make rhymes
By expressing what's on my mind
Like corrupt police
In almost every precinct
Or why the elderly won't eat
Or why kids get beat
With tears now in my eyes, I'm still going to keep on writing
You can judge me for the words I speak
Or you can respect me the more you read
Because I'm here when ever you're in need
Like a modern day Mr. Deed's
I hope my words touch you
I hope my poems can influence you
So keep on reading, and I will keep on writing...peace.

Printed in the United States
131609LV00001B/40/A